THE FALAISE GAP BATTLES
NORMANDY 1944

Simon Forty

Casemate
PHILADELPHIA & OXFORD

Published in the United States of America and Great Britain in 2017
by CASEMATE PUBLISHERS
1950 Lawrence Road, Havertown, PA 19083
and 10 Hythe Bridge Street, Oxford, OX1 2EW

ISBN-13: 978-1-61200-538-6
Produced by Greene Media Ltd.

Cataloging-in-publication data is available from the Library of Congress
and the British Library.

10 9 8 7 6 5 4 3 2 1

Printed and bound in China
For a complete list of Casemate titles please contact:
CASEMATE PUBLISHERS (US)
Telephone (610) 853-9131, Fax (610) 853-9146
E-mail: casemate@casematepublishers.com

CASEMATE PUBLISHERS (UK)
Telephone (01865) 241249, Fax (01865) 794449
E-mail: casemate-uk@casematepublishers.co.uk

Acknowledgments

Most of the contemporary photos are from BattlefieldHistorian.com,
NARA College Park, MD, and the George Forty Library—thanks to all.
The modern photos are mainly by the author with other credits noted on
the photographs. If anyone is missing or incorrectly credited, apologies:
please notify the author through the publishers.

I'd like to thank Richard Charlton-Taylor for the photos on page 7, Leo
Marriott (aerial photos), Barry van Veen of STIWOT (Traces of War is
undoubtedly the best way of planning an intinerary around the key sites), Mark
Franklin (maps), Ian Hughes (design concept), Richard Wood and the military
cyclists (particularly Peter Anderson) for photos and enthusiasm, and Steve
Smith for text improvements.

I'd also like to thank Wojtek Deluga for assistance at the The Polish Institute
and Sikorski Museum - London. The photos from their archive (at the back end
of the book) are credited PISM.

Preceding page:

Documents from the Inspector-General
of Panzer Troops show losses of 245
tanks—including this PzKpfw V Panther—
and assault guns in June 1944 in the west,
351 in July, 210 in August and 1,655 in
September. Delayed reporting for the
losses in August meant most were placed
in September.

Below:

On the edge of Vimoutiers, this Tiger
belonged to 2./sPzAbt 101 (though there is
some debate about this). It ran out of fuel,
was disabled, and abandoned by its crew.
For more information on this vehicle, see
the May 1975 (issue 8) *After The Battle*
magazine.

Contents

Introduction 4

THE POCKET FORMS 10

Operation Cobra 12

Third Army Operational 14

Operation Bluecoat 16

Operation Lüttich 18

Operation Totalize 22

Third Army Advances 24

Operation Tractable 28

CLOSING THE POCKET 30

The Killing Floor 38

THE END 44

Canadian 4th Armoured Division 46

US 90th Infantry Division 50

Polish 1st Armoured Division 52

Tournai-sur-Dive 60

Cemeteries 62

Bibliography 64

Key to Map Symbols 64

Introduction

The ill-conceived thrust towards Mortain, Operation *Lüttich*, produced a salient that allowed the Allies to encircle the German forces. Part of the reason for this was the speed with which Third Army was able to exploit the hole created by Operation Cobra. Against little opposition, Patton's armored spearheads reached Le Mans by August 9.

B Y THE LAST WEEK OF JULY 1944, the Allies had been cooped up in Normandy for seven weeks. They had invaded successfully, broken through the Atlantic Wall, and had taken Cherbourg and the north end of the Cotentin Peninsula. But then they hit trouble: in the west, the bocage countryside; in the east, in-depth antitank defenses and massed armor. The weather had been awful and the Press was growing impatient. Why was nothing happening? Omar Bradley's biography catches the mood, quoting a correspondent blaming the Allied gound forces' commander, Bernard Montgomery, for playing it safe and the US forces for following a policy "that costs the least number of lives."

The Allies did have a plan but they weren't telling the Press. From the start, as Bradley says, "Monty's primary task was to attract German troops to the British front that we might ... get into position for the breakout." And the breakout—Operation Cobra by Bradley's First Army—was just about to start.

In the east, to keep the Panzers away the British mounted a series of operations: Greenline, Pomegranate, Atlantic, Goodwood, and Spring all kept the Germans busy.

Cobra started badly with a weather delay on July 24 but the carpet-bombing on the 25th had its desired effect and created an opening that American armored spearheads quickly expanded. There was still heavy fighting, but by August 1, when Patton's Third Army became operational, the breach had widened and his men surged through. Against little effective opposition Patton's army advanced quickly, enhancing his reputation and giving the Press its field day.

Hitler then made a catastrophic decision: a counterattack to cut off Third Army and divide the US armies. Operation *Lüttich* started on August 6 and may have worked had his *Panzertruppen* been up to strength, but they had been blunted by the British and could muster nowhere near enough men and tanks to cause a significant problem. All the counterattack did achieve was to extend the German neck into a noose, which the Allies now proceeded to pull tight. Four Allied armies—Canadian First, British Second, and US First and Third—trapped what remained of the German defenders in a pocket and destroyed them.

The Germans fought like tigers to escape and were able to extricate more men than perhaps they should have done—a controversy that lingers to this day—but they did so without their heavy weapons, leaving behind at least 10,000 dead and around 50,000 prisoners. The battle for Normandy had ended in complete victory for the Allies who had out-thought and out-fought the German army. It was a brilliant example of Allied cooperation and should be remembered as such.

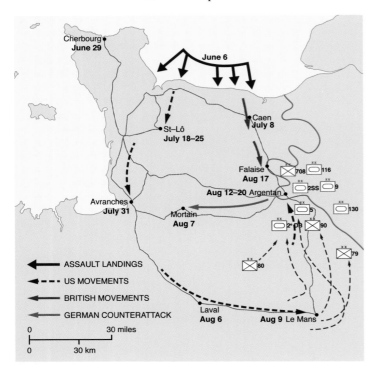

Cherbourg
June 29

June 6

St-Lô
July 18–25

Caen
July 8

Falaise
Aug 17   708   116
Aug 12–20 Argentan   2SS   9

Avranches
July 31   5   130

Mortain
Aug 7   2 DB   90

                            79

                  80

Laval
Aug 6   Aug 9 Le Mans

◄■ ASSAULT LANDINGS

◄- - - US MOVEMENTS

◄─ BRITISH MOVEMENTS

◄─ GERMAN COUNTERATTACK

0 ————— 30 miles

0 ————— 30 km

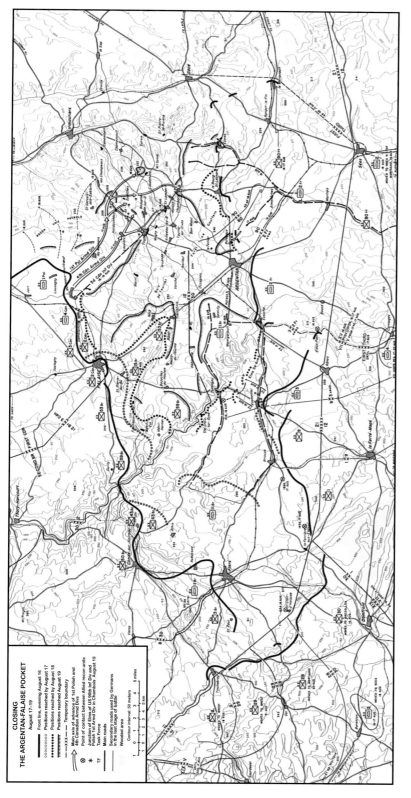

CLOSING
THE ARGENTAN-FALAISE POCKET
August 17-19

▬▬▬▬	Front line, evening August 16
◦◦◦◦◦◦◦	Positions reached by August 17
●●●●●●●	Positions reached by August 18
⋎⋎⋎⋎⋎⋎⋎	Positions reached August 19
—XXX—	Temporary boundary
⟶	Main axis of advance of 1st Polish and 4th Canadian Armd Divs
⊗	Point of contact between Allied recon units
✱	Junction of elms of US 90th Inf Div and Polish 1st Armd Div in Chambois August 19
TF	Task Force
▬▬▬▬	Main roads
═════	Secondary roads used by Germans in the last stage of battle
	Wooded area
	Contour interval: 50 meters

1 0 1 2 3 4 5 miles
1 0 1 2 3 4 5 km

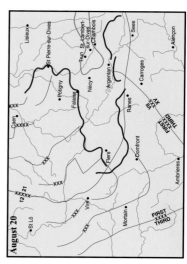

August 20

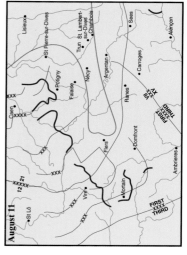

August 11

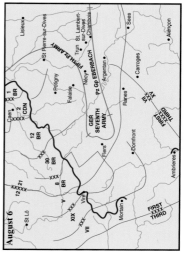

August 6

ALLIED GROUND FORCES IN NORMANDY (early August)

Supreme Allied Commander of the Allied Expeditionary Force: Gen. Dwight D. Eisenhower
Deputy Supreme Commander: Air Chief Marshal Sir Arthur Tedder
Commander Land Forces: Gen. Sir Bernard Montgomery

21st Army Group (Gen. Bernard Montgomery)

Canadian First Army (Lt Gen. "Harry" Crerar)
- I (BR) Corps (Lt Gen. John T. Crocker): BR 51st (Highland) Inf, 6th AB, and 49th (West Riding) Inf divisions.
- II Canadian Corps (Lt Gen. Guy G. Simonds): 1st Polish Armd, 4th Can Armd, 2nd Can Inf, 3rd Can Inf, and divisions plus 2nd Can Armd and 33rd (BR) Armd brigades.

BR Second Army (Lt Gen. Sir Miles Dempsey)
- VIII Corps (Lt Gen. Sir Richard N. O'Connor): Guards Armd, 11th Armd, and 15th (Scottish) Inf divisions plus 6th Guards Tk Bde attached 15th Div.
- XII Corps (Lt Gen. Neil M. Ritchie): 53rd (Welsh) Inf and 59th (Staffs) Inf divisions with 31st and 34th Tk brigades
- XXX Corps (Lt Gen. Gerard C. Bucknall; replaced in August by Lt Gen. Brian G. Horrocks): 7th Armd, 43rd (Wessex) Inf, and 50th (Northumbrian) Inf divisions plus 8th Armd Bde.

Twelfth Army Group (Gen. Omar Bradley)

US First Army (Gen. Courtney H. Hodges)
- V Corps (Maj Gen. Leonard T. Gerow): 2nd Inf Div.
- VII Corps (Maj Gen. J. Lawton Collins): 2nd Armd, 3rd Armd, 1st Inf, 4th Inf, 9th Inf, and 30th Inf divisions.
- XIX Corps (Maj Gen Charles H. Corlett): 28th Inf and 29th Inf divisions.

US Third Army (Gen George S. Patton, Jr.)
- VIII Corps (Maj Gen Troy H. Middleton—4th and 6th Armd, 8th and 83rd Inf divisions
- XV Corps (Maj Gen Wade H. Haislip): French 2nd Armd (2e DB), 5th Armd, 79th Inf, and 90th Inf divisions.
- XX Corps (Maj Gen Walton H. Walker): 7th Armd (from August 10), 5th Inf, and 80th Inf divisions.
- XII Corps (Maj Gen. Gilbert Cook, then Maj Gen. Manton Eddy): 4th Armd and 35th Inf divisions

Battle Casualties

Overall, the battle of Normandy saw German casualties of c. 450,000 men, of whom 240,000 were killed or wounded. The Allies had 209,672 casualties among the ground forces, including 36,976 killed and 19,221 missing. 21st Army Group suffered 83,000 British, Canadian and Polish troop casualties, of whom almost 16,000 were killed.

Analysis of casualties for the Falaise Gap battles is a surprisingly contentious issue and often depends on whether the author is trying to support the "they all got away" school of thought. It's also difficult to differentiate—particularly in German reports—between casualties and missing because of the confusion that saw many units only beginning to put correct figures in place in August. This accounts for the bulge in, for example, German tank losses, most of which were recorded in September rather than when they occurred in July/August. The concensus seems to be that around 80,000–100,000 German troops were caught in the encirclement. Some 10,000–15,000 of these were killed, 40,000–50,000 were taken prisoner, and 20,000–50,000 escaped—although the "escaped" figure runs as high in some accounts as 100,000.

The battle had also cost the Allies dearly. The Poles had 5,150 casualties in total, of which with 1,290 were killed; of these, 2,300 were for 1st Armored Division who had nearly 500 dead. Throughout the Normandy campaign, the Canadians suffered 18,444 casualties—7,415 between 1 and 23 August. From 8 until 21 August 1,479 were killed or died of wounds, 4,023 wounded or injured, and 177 captured.

US Army casualties for Northern France from July 25 to September 14 were 59,501, of which 17,844 died, 49,919 were wounded and 1,925 were missing.

Above:
The battle of Normandy had seemed to pit an unstoppable force against an immovable object. For nearly two months after D-Day the Germans held on, but the attrition and superior Allied strategic grasp of the battlefield finally paid off. But, even though in disarray, the Germans were still able to set up effective defenses.

Left:
The German army had many, many more horses than vehicles and thousands of them died in the reatreat.

1. Noyers-Bocage Typhoon memorial
2. Carpiquet Operation Windsor memorial
3. Hill 112 memorial
4. Banneville-la-Campagne CWGC cemetery
5. Mont Pinçon memorial
6. Boulon Don Mason Typhoon pilot memorial
7. Bretteville-sur-Laize Canadian cemetery
8. Grainville-Langannerie Polish cemetery
9. Worthington Force memorial
10. Falaise then and now signage
11. Habloville memorial
12. Flers 11th Armd Div memorial
13. Aubusson 11th Armd Div and King's Shropshire Lt Inf memorial
14. Vimoutiers Tiger I
15. Mont-Ormel memorial and museum
16. Coudehard memorial
17. Coudehard church
18. Trun memorial
19. Saint-Lambert-sur-Dive viewpoint
20. Saint-Lambert-sur-Dive Currie memorial
21. Saint-Lambert-sur-Dive German AA gun
22. Moissy ford
23. Tournai-sur-Dive Liberation Memorial
24. Aubry-en-Exmes church and sign
25. Aubry-en-Exmes von Richthofen memorial
26. Chambois Falaise Gap memorial
27. Chambois Allied meeting point memorial
28. Écouché M4 Massaoua Liberation Memorial
29. La Vieux Montmerrei M4 Keren memorial
30. Fleuré 2e DB Liberation Memorial
31. Towards Alençon (2e DB memorials)

Bayeux
Carpiquet
Noyers-Bocage
Vieux
Armayé-sur-O
R. Orne
Curcy-sur-Orne
Thury-Harcourt
Clécy
Condé-sur-Noireau
St
Flers

Left and Far left: Past and present views of a roadside shrine outside Fresnay-le-Puceux. The despatch rider is on a Norton 16H.

THE POCKET FORMS

Below right and Below:
It's a long way from Falaise, but this memorial (**below right**) to the Canadians at Carpiquet airport signifies the pressure placed on the German forces around Caen. They held the panzers in place to allow the breakout in the west. The knocked out Sherman and wrecked hangars are evidence of the fighting.

Far right and Opposite:
The pressure cooker around Caen saw the beautiful medieval city all but destroyed by Allied bombing and artillery.

Hitler ordered Generalfeldmarschall Günther von Kluge, *Oberbefehlshaber West* (Supreme Commander West) to counterattack the American breakout. The culmination of the Allied strategy in Normandy, Operation Cobra saw Bradley's First Army break out of the deadlock it had endured in the bocage country south of Carentan and unleash Third Army to exploit the gap. Initially, that exploitation was aimed at clearing the Brittany peninsula: very quickly it turned into a race for the Seine.

In the event, while Operation *Lüttich* made some inroads, it was checked by staunch US resistance, astute redistribution of troops by Bradley, and the paucity of German Panzers, most of which—including all the Tigers—were tied up against the British and Canadians around Caen. The German attack had, however, created the opportunity for the Allies to envelop the German armies in a pincer movement. 11th Armoured and British Second Army, along with US First Army, squeezed the western edges of the pocket that formed as Patton swung north to take Alençon and head towards Argentan. In the north, Canadian Second Army launched operations Totalize and Tractable to form the northern pincer.

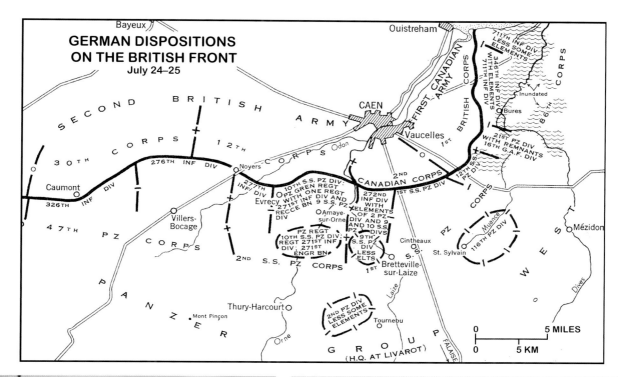

**GERMAN DISPOSITIONS
ON THE BRITISH FRONT**
July 24–25

11

Operation Cobra

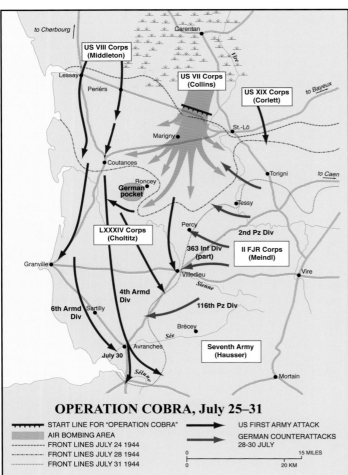

OPERATION COBRA, July 25–31

- ⊢⊢⊢⊢ START LINE FOR "OPERATION COBRA"
- ▓ AIR BOMBING AREA
- ----- FRONT LINES JULY 24 1944
- ----- FRONT LINES JULY 28 1944
- ······ FRONT LINES JULY 31 1944
- ➤ US FIRST ARMY ATTACK
- ➤ GERMAN COUNTERATTACKS 28-30 JULY

0 _____ 15 MILES
0 _____ 20 KM

AFTER A FALSE START ON JULY 24, Operation Cobra started off with carpet-bombing by 1,500 heavy bombers of the USAAF's Eighth Air Force. This certainly destroyed the German front lines: three battalion command posts of Panzer Lehr were demolished and the attached parachute regiment disappeared. The trouble was that it was indiscriminate, and short bombing accounted for several hundred American soldiers including Gen. Lesley McNair.

While distressing, the short bombing did not significantly hinder the American attack which quickly prospered. The Germans were able to scramble a strong defense on the eastern flank, but towards the sea a corridor opened up. On the 26th, VII Corps took Marigny, and VIII Corps moved across the Lessay–Périers road; by the 29th XIX Corps was advancing towards Torigni-sur-Vire and Tessy-sur-Vire, VII Corps had reached Percy, and VIII Corps was across the Sienne pushing on to Granville.

The Germans counterattacked around Percy, but could not stop the advance to Avranches and subsequently to Pontaubault and the bridge that was the key to Brittany. Bradley's attack had proved to be a masterstroke.

1

Opposite:
The American advance gathered speed after the first day and the Roncey pocket formed. Men of 3rd Armored study a Sturmgeschütz IIIG.

Above left and Left:
Devastation in the Roncey pocket, near St. Denis-le-Gast, July 31. The carcasses of a Schwimmwagen and a Marder.

Left and Below left:
Marigny was liberated on July 27 by 18th Inf Regt of 1st Inf Div as CCB of 3rd Armored and the Big Red One headed the thrust toward Countances. Note the *10.5 cm leichte Feldhaubitze 18* below the **1**—it would have come from one of Panzer Lehr's artillery regiments. Today, the scene is rather more pastel-colored.

13

Third Army Operational

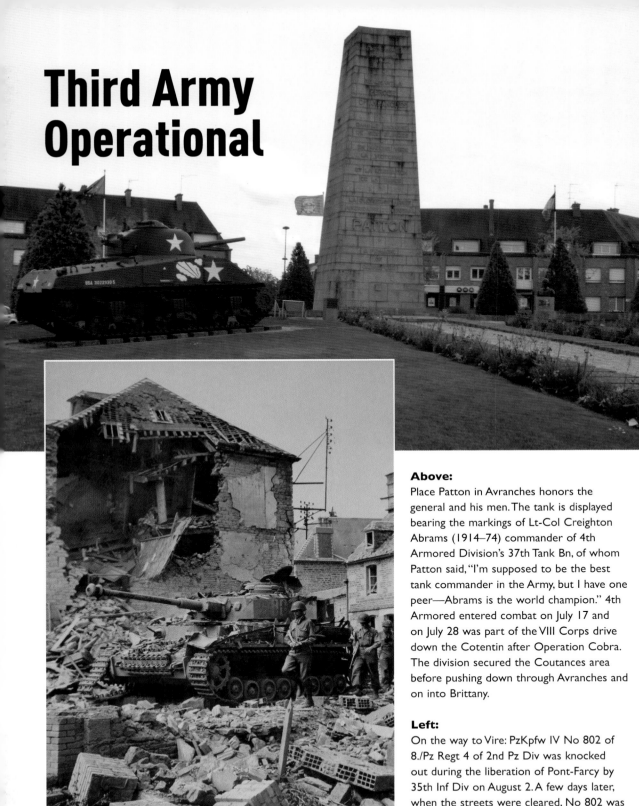

Above:
Place Patton in Avranches honors the general and his men. The tank is displayed bearing the markings of Lt-Col Creighton Abrams (1914–74) commander of 4th Armored Division's 37th Tank Bn, of whom Patton said, "I'm supposed to be the best tank commander in the Army, but I have one peer—Abrams is the world champion." 4th Armored entered combat on July 17 and on July 28 was part of the VIII Corps drive down the Cotentin after Operation Cobra. The division secured the Coutances area before pushing down through Avranches and on into Brittany.

Left:
On the way to Vire: PzKpfw IV No 802 of 8./Pz Regt 4 of 2nd Pz Div was knocked out during the liberation of Pont-Farcy by 35th Inf Div on August 2. A few days later, when the streets were cleared, No 802 was pushed out of the way.

It must have been frustrating! Gen. George Patton, Jr. had been sidelined for eleven months since the notorious August 1943 slapping incidents in Sicily. Bradley had been given command of the US forces in Normandy and Patton had been relegated to command of the phantom First US Army Group, part of the hugely succcessful Operation Fortitude deception that kept German forces in the Pas de Calais awaiting the "main" Allied invasion. While Patton's postwar reputation has over-egged the importance of his role in this deception, the Germans certainly fell for the operation hook, line, and sinker.

All good things, however, come to those that wait, and in July his real command, Third Army, moved from England to the Cotentin peninsula. On August 1, the army became operational and Patton's march to glory started.

The ground had been prepared for him by his old subordinate, Omar Bradley, whose First Army had endured the bad weather and the bocage, before breaking through the German defenses. Like the body-blows of a heavyweight boxer, First Army had sapped their opponent's strength and when the opening came, the knockout blow was swift and deadly.

Spearheaded by the 4th and "Super Sixth" Armored Divisions, Third Army might have been untested in war before Normandy, but it quickly showed itself to be an effective and flexible fighting force with three significant advantages as well as its dynamic, thrusting leader: close liaison with XIX Tactical Air Command, under Otto P. Weyland, provided exemplary reconnaissance and firepower; Col. Walter J. Muller proved a remarkable logistics supremo; and Col. Oscar W. Koch—helped by ULTRA—provided Patton with intelligence services second to none.

The stage was set for the Allies to throw off the shackles that had restrained them for so long.

Above left:
Third Army left England and made camp around Néhou. Today "Camp Patton" boasts this Sherman and other memorials.

Above:
On August 1 George Patton's Third Army became operational. He was the perfect general to exploit the hole in the German defenses.

Below:
A KO'd StuG III Ausf. G in Quettreville-sur-Sienne north of Granville.

Operation Bluecoat

Above and Above right:
The so-called "Charge of the Bull"—a reference to 11th Armoured's bull insignia—started on July 30 when it took Saint Martin des Besaces. Recon units discovered a surviving bridge over the Souleuvre River and the rampant division charged over, liberating Le Bény Bocage on August 1. The division advanced southward but had to withstand counterattacks from August 5 by 9th SS-Pz Div (Hohenstaufen), elements of 21st Pz Div, and the Tigers of s.SS-Pz Abt 102.

Wɪᴛʜ Oᴘᴇʀᴀᴛɪᴏɴ Cᴏʙʀᴀ in full swing, the Germans moved 2nd Panzer Division out of the defensive line against the British to become part of the armored force that would spearhead Operation *Lüttich*. This didn't provide much for the operation—2nd Panzer was down to its last twenty-five tanks by then—but it did create a hole opposite Caumont.

Operation Bluecoat started on July 30. Two corps, VIII and XXX, were involved—the former under Maj-Gen. "Pip" Roberts, probably Britain's most dynamic commander, the latter led by Lt-Gen. Gerard Bucknall who would lose his position after the operation. The plan was for VIII Corps to guard the flank and keep in touch with American forces advancing towards Vire while XXX Corps, headed by 7th Armoured Division, attacked towards Villers-Bocage, Mont Pinçon, and Thury-Harcourt.

In fact XXX Corps' attack bogged down, and it was Pip Roberts' 11th Armoured Division that made the inroads deep into German territory. The "Charge of the Bull" saw the division take Le Bény Bocage, capture an intact bridge over the Souleuvre River, and close on Vire before German reinforcements could shore up the defenses. Had the division been allowed to continue down the Vire road, the city might have fallen some days before it did on August 7. However, it was in the American zone, 11th Armoured were warned off and the chance was lost—instead they pushed east and took the highest point in the area, Mont Pinçon.

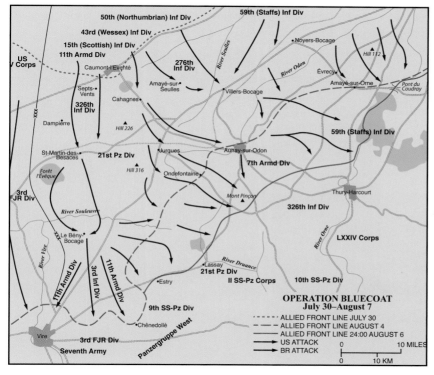

OPERATION BLUECOAT
July 30–August 7

- - - - - - ALLIED FRONT LINE JULY 30
- - - - ALLIED FRONT LINE AUGUST 4
———— ALLIED FRONT LINE 24:00 AUGUST 6
➤ US ATTACK
➤ BR ATTACK

0   10 MILES

0   10 KM

Map labels: 50th (Northumbrian) Inf Div; 59th (Staffs) Inf Div; 43rd (Wessex) Inf Div; Noyers-Bocage; 15th (Scottish) Inf Div; 11th Armd Div; Hill 112; US V Corps; Caumont-l'Eventé; 276th Inf Div; River Seulles; River Odon; Évrecy; Septs-Vents; Amayé-sur-Seulles; Villers-Bocage; Amayé-sur-Orne; Pont du Coudray; Cahagnes; 326th Inf Div; Dampierre; Hill 226; St-Martin-des-Besaces; 21st Pz Div; Jurques; Aunay-sur-Odon; 59th (Staffs) Inf Div; Forêt l'Évêque; Hill 316; Ondefontaine; 7th Armd Div; Thury-Harcourt; 3rd FJR Div; River Souleuvre; Mont Pinçon; 326th Inf Div; River Orne; Le Bény Bocage; LXXIV Corps; River Vire; 11th Armd Div; 3rd Inf Div; 11th Armd Div; River Druance; Lassay; 21st Pz Div; II SS-Pz Corps; 10th SS-Pz Div; Estry; 9th SS-Pz Div; Chênedollé; Vire; 3rd FJR Div; Seventh Army; Panzergruppe West

Above:

It's not often you knock out a Tiger II with a two-inch mortar, but that's what happened on August 7 at Le Plessis Grimoult. A platoon of A Co, 5th Duke of Cornwall's Light Infantry, discovered two of the Tigers in the process of bombing up. A mortar round hit the ammunition lorry which exploded, causing the tank's Porsche turret to be dislodged when, in turn, its ammunition exploded. The other Tiger scarpered.

Below left:

Mont Pinçon, rising to around 1,200 feet on the northwestern edge of the Suisse Normande, dominates the area. Defended by 276th and 326th Infantry Divisions, with LXXIV Panzer Corps also nearby, on August 6 two troops of 13th/18th Hussars drove to the summit and held it until the arrival of the rest of the regiment. The next day they were joined by 129th Infantry Brigade—4th Somersets and the Wiltshires—who were able to push the remaining Germans off the hill. After more heavy fighting they took Le Plessis Grimault, on the Southern slopes.

Operation Lüttich

Above:
The view from atop Hill 314 shows how good it was for artillery spotting—and the hard-pressed defenders were saved by the accuracy of the fire called down. Under the leadership of Capt. Reynold C. Erichson, who assumed command of the surrounded 2d Battalion, 120th Infantry, the troops on the hill for five days denied the Germans possession of terrain that would have given them observation over the major part of the VII Corps sector.

Above right:
Memorial to the 30th Inf Division on Hill 314 above Mortain.

Right:
Communications were crucial during the battle for Hill 314. At the end of the 6th, near St. Barthelemy, the Germans overran two companies of Lt-Col. Walter M. Johnson's 117th Infantry, and threatened to engulf the regimental command post. Johnson stayed at his post to direct the battle. The fighting was hard: one battalion of the 117th Infantry lost 350 men on August 7.

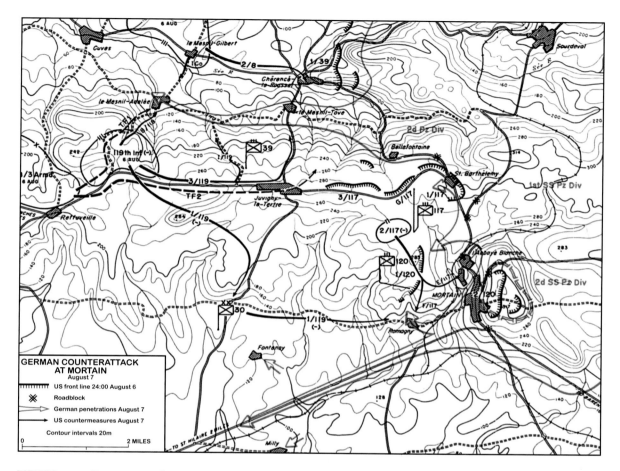

GERMAN COUNTERATTACK AT MORTAIN
August 7

	US front line 24:00 August 6
⊗	Roadblock
→	German penetrations August 7
→	US countermeasures August 7
	Contour intervals 20m

0   2 MILES

Wʜɪʟᴇ Oᴘᴇʀᴀᴛɪᴏɴ Lüᴛᴛɪᴄʜ can certainly be called ill-conceived, strategically it is easy to see why Hitler and his staff on the Eastern Front—already losing touch with the realities of the situation in France—wanted to counterattack. Had they had the forces to hand to reach the sea near Avranches they would—as Bradley points out in his autobiography—confine First Army to the hedgerows of the bocage, which suited the defenders, and cut twelve US divisions off from their supplies of gas and ammunition.

The trouble was, they didn't have the forces they needed to achieve this—but no matter that the German generals in Normandy knew the realities and were suggesting they pull back to a more suitably defensive line along the Seine as Montgomery expected, Hitler ordered von Kluge to strike. "That decision," Bradley avers, "more than any other, was to cost the enemy the Battle for France."

ULTRA warned Bradley of the counterattack, but it did so too close to the event for an immediate response. In the dawn light, and under cover of a morning mist that enveloped the area for some hours, the Germans made good initial progress. They were held up by 2/120th Infantry of 30th Division—the "Tough 'Ombres." They would win a Presidential Unit Citation for their valor. Bradley also assigned Third Army's 35th Infantry Division to Hodges' First Army to plug the holes in the defense.

Bradley held back four of the divisions that had passed through Avranches. Had they been needed they could have reinforced at Mortain; instead, they were flung east to form the lower edge of a pincer movement that would create the Falaise Pocket.

Above:

The German attacks at Mortain: note the island position of Hill 314 encircled by 2nd SS-Pz Div. Once the morning fog had lifted Allied air superiority saw the German positions attacked voraciously by fighter-bombers and pounded by artillery directed from the high points of Hill 314. Only 150 German tanks took part in this armored thrust, and fewer than 120 were saved.

Above:
Wounded of 2nd Bn, 120th Inf Regt of 30th Inf Div on Hill 314 at a 105th Medical Battalion Aid Station.

Below:
Tanks of E Co, 67th Armd Regt (2nd Armored Div). Bradley's adroit handling of the forces in the area saw, less than twenty-four hours after the Germans attacked, VII Corps' strength increased to seven divisions—five infantry and two armored.

Right:
The battle around the White Abbey, a nunnery near Le Neufbourg/Mortain railway station, pitted F Coy, 2nd Bn, 120th Inf Regt and the 3in towed antitank guns of 1st Pl, A Coy, 823rd TD Bn against 9./SS-PzGr Regt 4 *Der Führer* and elements of 2nd SS-Pz Div (*Das Reich*). Six German SdKfz 251 APCs were KO'd as well as *Schwimmwagen* (amphibious jeeps) and *Kübelwagen*.

Operation Totalize

Above:

Memorial to the brave men of Worthington Force, decimated by 12th SS-Pz Div *Hitlerjugend* supported by Tigers of sSS-PzAbt 101 and Panthers of SS-Pz Regt 12. They were ordered to take Hill 195 by night attack on August 9 but ended up four miles off-track and, therefore, unable to call down fire support. By the time their position was discovered, rescue attempts ran into heavy fire and were unable to relieve them. They were eventually overwhelmed, losing 44 vehicles and over 200 men, although some small units and, amazingly, four tanks were able to escape: Their objective, Hill 195, was taken on August 10 by the 1st Argyll and Sutherlands—by night attack.

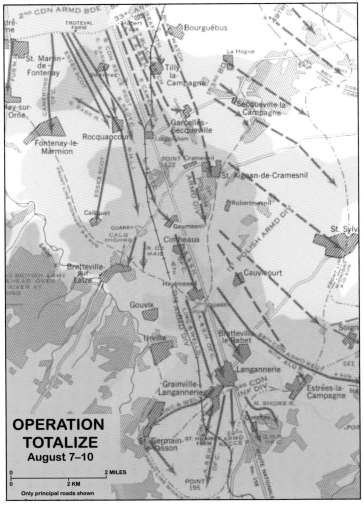

OPERATION TOTALIZE
August 7–10

0   2 MILES
0   2 KM
Only principal roads shown

Around Caen it was business as usual. The Germans' defenses were stacked five miles deep. While their air assets were, for all purposes, out of the battle, the ground forces still maintained a stranglehold. New measures were called for, and Lt-Gen. Guy Simonds, commanding Canadian II Corps, had an idea.

Today we are used to "battle taxis"—armored personnel carriers (APCs) or infantry fighting vehicles—in 1944 it was a new concept. Simonds had the weapons taken out of his M7 Priest SP guns and converted them into Kangaroo APCs. Later, Canadian Ram tanks were used.

Lining up in six columns, the Canadian troops advanced behind a rolling artillery barrage and dismounted 200 yards from their objectives. Soon, they had taken Verrières Ridge, which had cost over 4,000 casualties in earlier attacks.

Unfortunately, the second phase of the operation, conducted by the inexperienced Polish 1st and Canadian 4th Armoured divisions, took too long to get started and was stymied by a *Hitlerjugend* counterattack assisted by Michael Wittmann and the Tigers of heavy SS-Panzer Battalion 101. It was during this attack that Joe Ekins of the 1st Northamptonshire Yeomanry knocked out four tanks—including three Tigers, one of which may have been Wittman's.

Left and Below:
Then and now pairs showing:
1 Rocquancourt, where there is a memorial to the Canadian liberators.
2 May-sur-Orne, where the damaged church was completely replaced postwar.
3 Cintheaux, just south of the Canadian cemetery at Bretteville-sur-Laize.

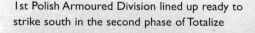
1st Polish Armoured Division lined up ready to strike south in the second phase of Totalize

Third Army Advances

Below:
A halftrack of the 41st Armd Inf Regt (2nd Armd Div) enters Lonlay L'Abbaye. It was part of CCA which passed through on August 14.

Opposite:
An M4 of 67th Armd Regt of 2nd Armd Div patrols Domfront on August 14.

The speed of third army's advance after breaking out of the Avranches corridor was breathtaking, particularly when compared to the two months that had gone before, and the progress of the Canadians and Poles towards Falaise. In fact, of course, it's like comparing chalk and cheese: Operation Totalize saw significant defensive forces including Tigers; Patton's attack cut through areas that were, if not devoid of Nazis, then certainly devoid of any significant defenses.

With the Mortain counterattack held, and USAAF and RAF fighter-bombers pounding what was left of the attacking forces, Bradley ordered Patton to get his forces moving—he didn't have to ask twice.

Troy Middleton's VIII Corps was already fanning out in Brittany. It had reached Saint-Malo and Rennes on August 4, and Brittany and Lorient by August 7—although Saint-Malo held out until August 17 and Brest till September 18. Because of the casualties these two sieges incurred, Lorient was masked. It surrendered along with the rest of the ports on May 10, 1945.

Walton Walker's XX Corps was guarding the south flank of the army. It passed that job onto XII Corps on August 13, moving then to Chartres (August 15), heading towards the Seine–Orléans gap. It reached Fontainebleau on the 23rd.

Wade Haislip's XV Corps had taken Mayenne on August 5, Laval on the 7th, and Le Mans on the 8th. It was ordered to move north from Le Mans towards Argentan on the axis Le Mans–Alençon–Sées. Carrouges was taken by 2e DB, while the 5th Armored took Sées, before both drove towards Argentan, arriving there on August 13 (although the city didn't fall for another week). In doing so, they broke up a projected counterattack by Panzer Group Eberbach (see map opposite) before it could happen.

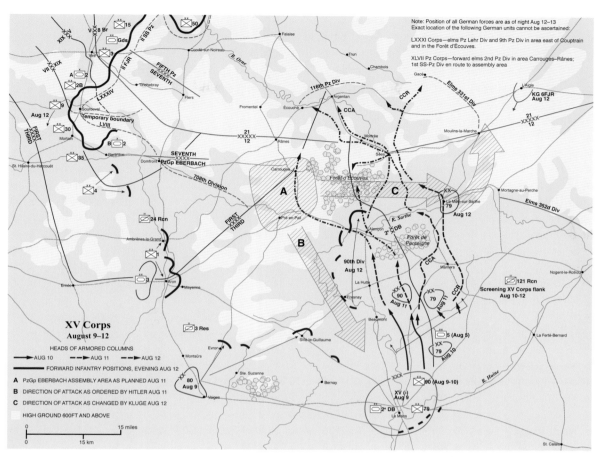

Note: Position of all German forces are as of night Aug 12–13
Exact location of the following German units cannot be ascertained:

LXXXI Corps—elms Pz Lehr Div and 9th Pz Div in area east of Couptrain
and in the Forêt d'Écouves.

XLVII Pz Corps—forward elms 2nd Pz Div in area Carrouges–Rânes;
1st SS-Pz Div en route to assembly area

XV Corps
August 9–12

HEADS OF ARMORED COLUMNS

→ AUG 10   - → AUG 11   -- → AUG 12

── FORWARD INFANTRY POSITIONS, EVENING AUG 12

A PzGp EBERBACH ASSEMBLY AREA AS PLANNED AUG 11

B DIRECTION OF ATTACK AS ORDERED BY HITLER AUG 11

C DIRECTION OF ATTACK AS CHANGED BY KLUGE AUG 12

▨ HIGH GROUND 600FT AND ABOVE

0 ——————— 15 miles
0 ——————— 15 km

25

1 This 2e DB M4A2, named *Valois*, was KO'd by 9th SS-Pz Div in the battle in the forest of Écouves, August 13. *Ikmoned/WikiCommons (CC BY-SA 4.0)*

2 *Massaoua*, an M4A2 of the 1st Coy of the 501ème RCC, 2e DB at Écouché. It was damaged in the battle for the town's liberation on August 13.

3 Another 501ème RCC M4A2, this one—*Keren*—at Le Vieux-Montmerrei, was knocked out in the fighting here on August 12.

4 This monument outside Alençon remembers the French General Leclerc and his 2nd Armored Division (2e DB), who fought their way to the city August 10–12.

5 Monument commemorating Leclerc in Alençon, inaugurated in 1970.

6 Leclerc's HQ in Alençon, opposite his memorial.

7 and 8 Then and now views of Alençon cathedral area.

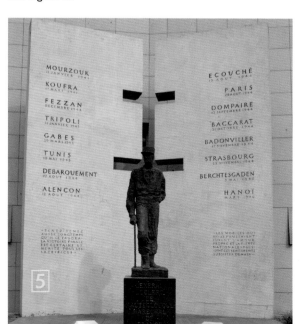

Operation Tractable

The northern pincer in the trap was formed by Canadian First Army which launched Operation Tractable on August 14. Unlike Totalize, the operation was to take place in daylight under cover of a smokescreen without an artillery precursor to use surprise to catch the Germans offguard. Again the attack would be concentrated narrowly in two columns, using APCs to carry the infantry, with feint attacks on August 12 and 13 to draw the enemy away from the main thrust.

Unfortunately, the element of surprise was missing: the Germans had captured notes about the attack from the body of a Canadian officer. The defenders—12th SS-Pz Div *Hitlerjugend* again—were able to place the bulk of their antitank defenses in exactly the right places. *Hitlerjugend* had suffered severely in the recent fighting and was spread thinly: being able to tailor their troop dispositions to the attack helped considerably and allowed the reduced division to hold up the Canadian advance.

The plan was to take Falaise the first day and then advance on Chambois and Trun, and initially things went well: the Laison river was crossed, but *Hitlerjugend* didn't give up an inch of ground without a fight and the attack slowed. By August 15 they were to the east of Falaise but the city was still in German hands. It would finally fall on the 18th, but by then the action had moved east to Chambois.

OPERATION TRACTABLE
August 14–16

Front line, first light August 15 ---
Front line, midnight August 15–16 ••••••
Contours indicated by tints at 50, 100, and 150m

Opposite, Above:
Simonds converted around 60 Priests into APCs for Operation Totalize showing the way ahead for mobile infantry. Here they transport 1st Black Watch.

Opposite, Below:
Heavy fighting took place on August 14 along the Laison River, a major obstacle to the Canadians, until bridges could be laid as here at Rouvres.

Above:
The South Alberts were the first unit into Damblainville, east of Falaise, as the pocket's jaws narrowed.

Left: Fort Garry Horse Shermans await the start of Operation Tractable. It was part of Canadian 2nd Armd Bde which was grouped with 3rd Inf Div in the attack.

CLOSING THE POCKET

Past and present pairs of Falaise, liberated by Canadian troops on August 17, 1944. During its liberation Falaise was flattened, some seventy percent of buildings destroyed and hundreds of inhabitants killed—over 20,000 Normans died during the battles in 1944. They are remembered in Falaise in The Civilians in Wartime Memorial (*Mémorial des Civils de la Guerre*), a museum that opened in 2016.

THE DENOUEMENT OF THE BATTLE of Normandy, launched on a wing and a prayer on June 6, took place ten weeks later on August 18–21 in a small area between Chambois, Mont-Ormel, and St. Lambert-sur-Dive.

With the Canadian and Polish advance from the north sticking against a tenacious defense, and the so-called "Falaise Pocket" deflating like a burst balloon, it is surprising that the American forces in the south didn't force their way north. In fact, it was not until August 20 that XV Corps finally took Argentan and advanced towards Chambois to seal the pocket. By then the retreating Germans, squeezed from the west by US First and British Second Army, were fleeing helter-skelter but still in good order, towards the Polish positions on Mont-Ormel, where Polish 1st Armoured fought to their last round.

The reasons why the gap wasn't closed immediately are well outlined at the start of Chapter 26 in Martin Blumenson's *Breakout and Pursuit*: they boil down, as Bradley said, to the fact that he preferred "a solid shoulder at Argentan to a broken neck at Falaise." Seventy years on, the reasons tend to be discussed in more nationalistic terms, usually with the blame being passed to a general of a different nationality to the writer!

The reality is that the Germans, even in defeat, didn't allow their retreat to become a rout. They had become masters of this on the Eastern Front and the same would be true in the west. They were helped by the fanaticism of their soldiers and their authoritarian regime (over 4,000 German soldiers were executed in 1944 for desertion and other reasons), and by an understandable desire by the Allies to conserve their troops. In the end, the Allies had beaten an army that was experienced and motivated, and had had four years to prepare its defenses.

Left:
One of a series of Past and Present posters around Falaise that bring home the devastation the town suffered in 1944.

Argentan was the goal of Third Army's XV Corps which attacked northward on August 10, spearheaded by 5th Armd Div and Leclerc's 2e DB. 80th Inf Div liberated the city on the morning of August 20, delayed on Bradley's orders. It was a real baptism of fire for 80th Div (CG Maj-Gen Horace L. McBride) who had only arrived in France over Utah Beach on August 2.

Top, left and right:
Panther Ausf A of I. Abt Pz Regt 24 attached to 116 Pz Div. It's on rue Aristide Briand. II./Pz-Regt 33 of 9. Pz Div also defended Argentan.

Above left and Left:
Above and Top:
Classic view of 318th IR entering Argentan. The road sign, unfortunately, is no more.

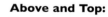

Above and Top:
Then and now views
of Argentan town
hall which had to be
knocked down and
rebuilt. Men of 318th
Inf Regt are raising the
American flag.

Left and Above:
Another August 20
photo of men from
318th Inf, here looking
over to the St. Germain
Church, a view obscured
by rebuilding today.

The pursuit of the Germans by US First Army and BR Second Army, the latter in the form of XXX Corps, ensured they couldn't set up a sufficiently strong defensive position to allow their forces to escape the pocket.

Opposite, Above and Below:
First Army heavy artillery at Lake Bagnoles de l'Orne. A Mack 7.5ton prime mover pulls an M1 155mm gun. The town was liberated on the night of August 13/14.

Above and Above left:
Couterne was liberated on August 13, between 21:00 and 24:00 by US 1st Inf Div.

Left:
A German 10.5cm leFH18 gun stands next to the war memorial in the village of Habloville where 10. SS-Pz-Div (Frundsberg) set up a strong blocking position on the night of August 17–18 and played a significant role in holding up the British. On August 18, Frundsberg relinquished Habloville, having fought to keep the mouth of the Falaise Pocket open.

After Operation Bluecoat, the 11th Armoured Division was attached to XXX Corps. It progressed eastward snapping at the heels of the Germans, moving from the Villers-Bocage–Caen road through Aubusson and Flers (on August 17), to Putanges (**Right**) on August 19, and then through Argentan—once it had been taken—and Gacé to L'Aigle. They were, as Edgar W. I. Palamountain said in *Taurus Pursuant,* "the hammer, while the Americans, represented by 80th US Inf Div and 90th on their left, formed the anvil." The main memorial in France to the division (**opposite, below**) is at Pont de Vère.

Above and Left: Vassy fell to XXX Corps on August 14 when the 4th Battalion, King's Shropshire Light Infantry, part of 11th Armoured Division's 159th Infantry Brigade Group took it without a fight. Today the road entering the town is little changed although the hillside above is full of houses.

IN GRATEFUL MEMORY OF THE SOLDIERS OF THE 11TH ARMOURED DIVISION WHO GAVE THEIR LIVES IN NORMANDY AND ELSEWHERE IN EUROPE 1944 - 1945

The Killing Floor

1 Traffic jams as German transport flees the pocket.

2 and 3
Jagdgeschwader 2 "Richthofen," named for the famous Red Baron, numbered among its 10th Staffel's pilots Ruthard von Richthofen, a distant cousin of the great man. An *Oberfähnrich* (senior NCO), Ruthard died flying an Fw190A8 on July 13, 1944, when he was shot down by a P-51 Mustang near Argentan.

4 and 5 11th Armoured Division's advance eastward was briefly checked at Aubusson on August 16, before the village was taken by the King's Shropshire Light Infantry. This wooden Tommy and stone stele remember the battle

6, 7, and 8 In the aftermath of Operation *Lüttich* and the Falaise Gap battles there were claims that Allied airpower had been the crucial factor. Today we know that many of the German armor losses were down to adandonment as a result of automotive unreliability and lack of fuel. However, against men and soft-skinned vehicles the fighter-bombers were deadly. The fight was not entirely one-sided. German Flak over the battlefield was intense as is evinced by the memorial at Noyers Bocage (**8**) that is dedicated to the Typhoon pilots—over 150 of them—who died over Normandy, May–August 1944. One of them was Plt Off Donald William Mason, RAAF, seen (**Center left**) standing on the wing of his RAF No 198 Sqn Mk 1A Hawker Typhoon. He was shot down on June 18 near the village of Boulon. His body was exhumed in late 1992 and was buried with in the St Charles de Percy Calvados War Cemetery, France. There is a memorial to him at Boulon (**7**).

9 Vehicles knocked out from the air on the roads between Falaise and Argentan.

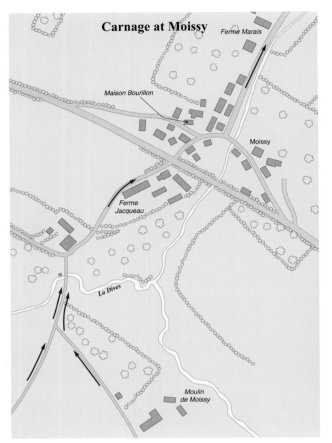

Carnage at Moissy

Ferme Marais

Maison Bourillon

Moissy

Ferme
Jacqueau

La Dives

Moulin
de Moissy

CIRCUIT AOÛT 44
DERNIÈRE BATAILLE DE NORMANDIE
Paysages et sites historiques classés au Patrimoine National Français

Chambois - Gué de Moissy

Above and Left:
Men unable to get to the bridges over the Dives tried to use the ford in the hamlet of Moissy. Today, a couple of adult-sized bounds take you across. The Dives is a ridiculously small river. But, in mid-August 1944, it was clogged with abandoned armor, wrecked machinery and corpses.

Top right and Center right:
Ferme Jacqueau at Moissy and the road from the ford were choked by abandoned vehicles and the dead, men and animals, mainly horses.

Below right:
Memorial at Trun to Canadian 4th Armoured Division. Realizing that the key to trapping the fleeing Germans was Trun, Gen Guy Simonds ordered the division to advance in that direction on August 16, and then to move on to St.-Lambert. The South Alberta Regiment, the divisional armored reconnaissance regiment, was in the forefront of the action.

RUE
DES
POLONAIS
1ÈRE D.B. POLONAISE

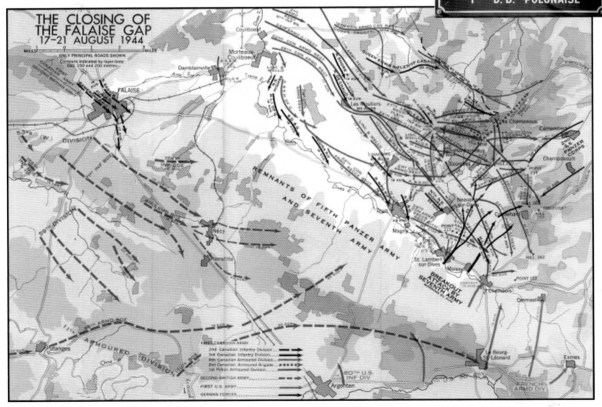

THE CLOSING OF
THE FALAISE GAP
17–21 AUGUST 1944

Far left:

Posed photo purporting to show the linkup between the US 359th Inf Regt, 90th Inf Div and Polish 10th Dragoons, 1st Armd Div in Chambois. In fact the linkup took place at 18:00 on August 19 between Capt. Laughlin E. Waters of Co G, 2/359th Inf Regt and Maj. W. Zgorzelski of 10th Polish Dragoons.

Left:

Tanks of Polish 1st Armoured enter Chambois along the aptly named rue des Polonnais. It leads from Mont Ormel. *PISM; inset Romain Bréget/WikiCommons*

Right:

The reconstructed church at Aubry-en-Exmes. It was destroyed in the fighting.

Inset, Below:

The Circuit Août 1944 board at Aubry looks at the plight of the German army horses. It identifies the total equine losses in the pocket as being 6,000–10,000, but Dinaldo's analysis in *Mechanized Juggernaut or Military Anachronism?: Horses and the German Army in WWII* puts the figure at nearer 40,000.

Below:

Two US soldiers, probably from 90th Inf Div, between Chambois and Fel during the fighting. This photograph is used on the Circuit Août 1944 boards.

THE END

Postwar, there has been criticism of the Allies for the number of German troops that escaped the trap. It wasn't the first time the Germans had managed to extricate numbers of men from a tricky siuation: they did so from Sicily, too. The professionalism of the German retreat from the Falaise Pocket, however, cannot hide the hard facts: within three months of D-Day, the Allies had exploded the myth of the Atlantic Wall, had destroyed the German armies in place in Normandy and those sent to support them, and would soon be knocking on the door of the Reich itself. While the Germans may have saved a good number of men, they had lost most of their heavy weapons and they had lost France.

Key to map
August 18:
1 The Canadians (3rd Inf and 4th Armd Divisions) capture Trun. The gap is around five miles wide.

2 Maj Currie's 4th Armd Div battlegroup takes Hill 117 and heads toward St.-Lambert.

3 The Polish 1st Armd Div takes heights above Coudehard overlooking the German escape route.

4 FR Groupe de Langlade of 2e DB advances on La Frênée to block the retreating Germans on Route 16, but turns back with orders to be ready to rush to liberate Paris, which they did on August 24th.

5 Elements of US 90th Inf Div move out of Argentan and recapture Le Bourg-St Léonard, providing artillery spotting locations from the ridge. They move on to attack Chambois and Fel.

August 19:
6 Can 4th Armd Div tries to link with US forces in Chambois.

7 Polish 1st Armd Div attacks towards the Americans around Chambois.

8 Polish 10th Mounted Rifles reach Chambois at 19:00 linking with US troops. but insufficient force to keep the pocket—holding remnants of fifteen German divisions—closed.

9 Gen Meindl's 3FJR (II Para Corps) holds left flank.

August 20:
10 12th SS-Pz Div HQ breaks out around 01:00.

11 Elements of XLVII Pz Corps and I SS Pz Corps break out under cover of darkness.

12 Canadian forces join up with American and Polish forces, temporarily sealing the gap.

13 German counterattacks to reopen the pocket. What remains of 2nd and 9th SS-Pz Divs attack the Poles from outside the pocket. The battles on Hill 262 from the night of August 19/20, are intense. Around midday elements of 10th SS, 12th SS, and 116th Pz divisions manage to escape.

August 21:
14 The night of 20/21 is the hardest for the beleaguered Poles, but elements of the Can 4th Armd arrive at dawn to relieve the pressure on Hill 262. Fighting stops in Chambois. 2,000 Germans surrender in Tournai-sur-Dive (see p. 60–61). The battle is effectively over.

Opposite and Above: Just outside St.-Lambert-sur-Dive, there's a viewpoint that looks down the main village street towards Moissy and Chambois.

Right: Circuit Août 44 board at St. Lambert—note our frontispiece photo.

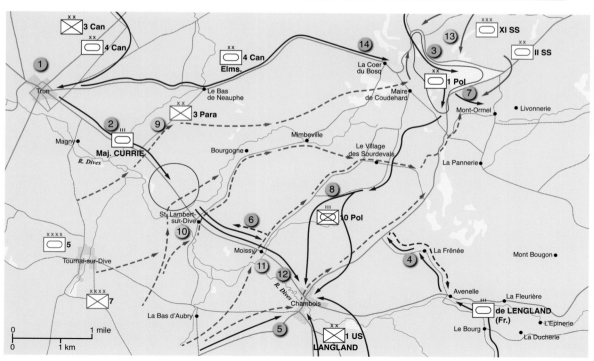

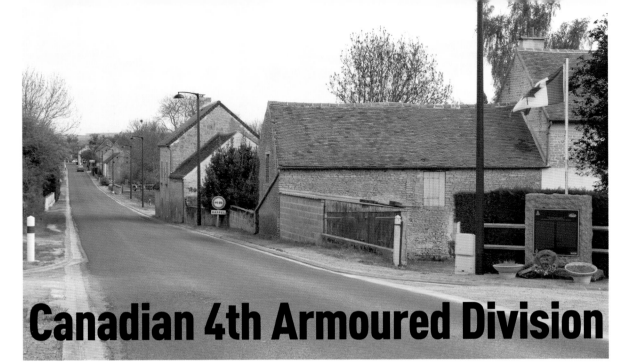

Canadian 4th Armoured Division

Opposite:
Photos from the main street of St.-Lambert, looking south. **Bottom right** shows David Currie (at left, holding revolver) who was awarded the VC for his valor during the fighting in the village on August 18–19. At right in the **Top** photo is the memorial to Maj. Currie who commanded a battle group made up of a squadron of The South Alberta Regiment, units of the 7th Bn, The Argyll and Sutherlands Highlanders, the Lincoln and Welland Regt, and the 5th Anti-tank Regt. They fought for three days to keep the Falaise pocket closed.

Above left:
Wary troops patrol the village.

Below left:
Generalleutnant Otto Elfeldt before his interrogation at St.-Lambert on August 20. Having commanded 47th Inf Div in Normandy, he commanded LXXXIV Armee Korps from July 1944. He was captured by Polish troops of 10th Cav Regt (Pulk Strzelcow Konnych) along with 29 officers of his staff. The American is from 701st TD Bn.

Above and Right:
KO'd Sherman V of 4th Trp, C Sqn of 29th Recce Regt (The South Alberta Regiment) of 4th Can Armd Div at St.-Lambert-sur-Dive on August 19. The infantry unit is B Coy, The Argyll and Sutherland Highlanders of Canada-Princess Louise. They are advancing towards Chambois. Note at right the destroyed PzKpfwIV.

Below:
St.-Lambert after the battle.

Above and Center left:
Knocked-out German armor on the outskirts of St.-Lambert. Fighting around the bridges in the village was intense. The Argylls, lacking explosives, had left the bridge intact when they were forced to withdraw in the face of infiltration across the entire front. Despite heavy casualties, they destroyed seven enemy tanks, twelve 88mm guns and 40 vehicles, and captured 2,100.

Left:
Flak 30 20mm German AA gun on display in the village.

US 90th Infantry Division

Right:
Men of the 90th Division exhibit the spoils of war in Chambois.

Below right:
Memorial commemorating the soldiers who fought in the Falaise Pocket in front of the 14th-century keep at Chambois.

Below:
Memorial to the meeting of Poles and Americans at Chambois. Note at left the insignia of the "Tough 'Ombres" and Polish 1st Armoured Division.

Bottom, Left and Right
Fel after the battle.

Right and Below:
A Canadian soldier helps a wounded German down from an SdKfz 251 halftrack used to ferry survivors to a US aid station in Fel. set up by the Regimental Medical Detachment) of 359th Infantry Regiment (90th Inf Div). Note the trident marking of 2nd Panzer Division on the back of the halftrack.

Polish 1st Armoured Division

Tʜᴇ ᴄᴏʀᴋ ɪɴ ᴛʜᴇ ʙᴏᴛᴛʟᴇ: Montgomery said that the Allies had caught the Germans in a bottle, and the Polish Armoured Division was the cork. Inside the bottle seethed the mass of German troops retreating as their hold on Normandy crumbled. Harried by fighter-bombers and the advancing troops of US First and British Second armies, the Germans were squeezed past the high ground of Mont Ormel (Hill 262) which sits high above the valley of the Dives. Atop this promontory sat Polish 1st Armoured. Their epic fight against the Germans trying to leave the pocket and the troops trying to break in to help them saw German losses of around 2,000 men killed, 5,000 taken prisoner and 55 tanks, 44 guns, and 152 other armored vehicles destroyed.

Isolated for three days in their positions on what they termed *Maczuga*— the Mace—the Poles, with their last ammunition expended, were finally relieved by 4th Canadian Armoured Brigade at midday on August 21. Polish 1st Armoured paid a high price: around twenty percent of the division's combat strength—over 300 dead and over 1,000 wounded and missing. In the campaign the casualties were some 1,500 including 466 dead.

The monument at the Mémorial de Montormel honors Polish 1st Armd Div (**1**), 2e DB (**2**), the 359th Inf Regt of US 90th Inf Div (**3**), the Canadian Grenadier Guards of the Can 4th Armd Div (**4**), and the French Resistance (**5**). The other badge is of 21st Army Group (**6**). Two armored vehicles are exhibited, a 2e DB M8 Greyhound and an M4A1(76) W Sherman named *Maczuga*.

Right:
Polish 1st Armoured Division's route to Mont Ormel.

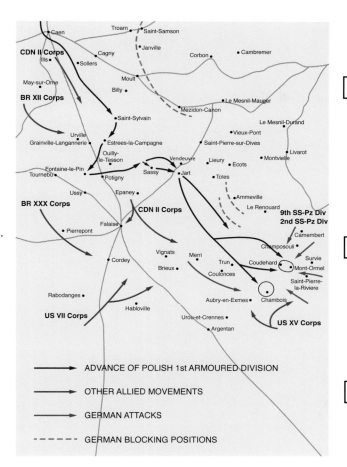

ADVANCE OF POLISH 1st ARMOURED DIVISION

OTHER ALLIED MOVEMENTS

GERMAN ATTACKS

GERMAN BLOCKING POSITIONS

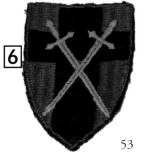

1 and 2 Views from and up to the Mémorial de Montormel shows graphically the German problems. The Poles were well-entrenched and the German attacks verged on the suicidal.

3 Knocked out PzKpfw IV. *PISM*

4 Polish troops dug in on the Mace. *PISM*

5 Polish troops survey the destruction rained down on the escaping Germans. *PISM*

6 Coudehard Church—Polish troops were entrenched around this area.

Right:
Two of the *Circuit Août 44* boards. All of them feature Past and Present photography.

Below:
Boisjois was an aid and command post during the fighting. It is little changed today. *PISM*

Left:
Memorial to the Polish actions on Hill 262.

Below left:
Panther and Sherman showing the proximity of the two sides during the fighting. *PISM*

Below:
The Poles lost eleven tanks on the Mace. Lt-Col. Aleksander Stefanowicz's 1st Armored Regt held on Hill 262 from August 19 to 21, with the night of 20/21 being particularly critical. "Tonight we will be dying for Poland and civilization," said the wounded Stefanowicz. They were relieved by the arrival of the Canadian Grenadier Guards at 14:00 on the 21st. *PISM*

Left:
Polish tankers after the fighting. *PISM*

Center left:
The crew of a Polish Sherman with their "trophy"—a Panther knocked out in the fighting. *PISM*

Bottom left:
KO'd Polish Sherman. *PISM*

Right:
Gen. Maczek (right) and Lt. Col. Ludwik Stankiewicz, his Chief of Staff. To his men he was "Baca"—a traditional Polish name for a shepherd—esteemed as a leader and as a man. After Poland fell, General Stanisław Maczek, then a colonel, escaped with the remnants of his brigade and, after a short time in France, ended up in Britain where Polish 1st Armd Div was formed. Their first taste of combat was in Operation Totalize and they acquitted themselves with courage and elan, as they did for the rest of hostilities—in particular around Mont Ormel as they fought to keep the Falaise Gap closed. Maczek's courage makes the British postwar treatment of him even more disgraceful: refused a pension he ended up working as a bartender. *PISM*

Stanisław Maczek
(1892 - 1994)

Generał Broni Wojska Polskiego
Dowódca I Dywizji Pancernej

Commander in Chief General des Forces Armées Polonaises
Commandant de la 1re Division Blindée

Lieutenant General of the Polish Armed Forces
Commander of the 1st Armoured Division

Tournai-sur-Dive

On August 21, 1944, Tournai-sur-Dive was the site of the surrender of a sizable body of Germans trapped in the Falaise Pocket in the baking July heat. Hounded by Allied bombs and artillery, as many as 2,000 German soldiers surrendered to the Canadians here as a result of negotiations assisted by the local priest, Father Launay. To commemorate this, and remember the many who died, there are a number of memorials in the town:

1 A bust of Father Marcel Launay (1910–1970) who played such an important role in the negotiations with the Germans for the cessation of hostilities.

2 M3 halftrack, in front of which a sign commemorates the surrender of 800 German soldiers.

3 Plaques on the church wall honor Flg Off Ron Currie, No 184 Sqn, RCAF who was shot down on August 18, 1944—he's buried in the Canadian cemetery at Bretteville-sur-Laize. A second plaque remembers civilian victims of the war.

4 Plaque commemorating the surrender of German troops in the farmyard behind between 14:30 and 17:00 on August 21.

3

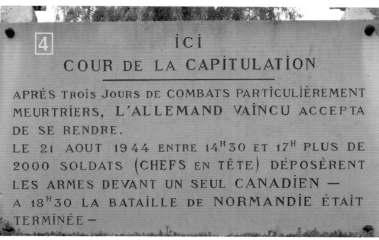

4

ICI
COUR DE LA CAPITULATION

APRÈS TROIS JOURS DE COMBATS PARTICULIÈREMENT
MEURTRIERS, L'ALLEMAND VAINCU ACCEPTA
DE SE RENDRE.
LE 21 AOÛT 1944 ENTRE 14ᴴ30 ET 17ᴴ PLUS DE
2000 SOLDATS (CHEFS EN TÊTE) DÉPOSÈRENT
LES ARMES DEVANT UN SEUL CANADIEN —
A 18ᴴ30 LA BATAILLE DE NORMANDIE ÉTAIT
TERMINÉE —

Below left:

The *Circuit Août 44* (Circuit August 1944)—ten panels spread round key places associated with the last battles in Normandy—was inaugurated at the Mont-Ormel Memorial in September 2013. At just over 10 miles long, the circuit passes through Chambois, Aubry-en-Exmes, Tournai-sur-Dive, the corridor of death through Saint-Lambert-sur-Dive and Bourgogne to La cour du Bosq (four boards)—with a side detour to the ford over the river at Moissy—Point 262 (the Polish marker) on the Mace at Coudehard, and back to the Mont Ormel Memorial.

Cemeteries

THEIR NAME LIVETH
FOR EVERMORE

1 The British CWGC cemetery of Banneville-la-Campagne contains 2,170 Commonwealth burials, 140 of them unidentified, and five Polish graves. Most were killed in the battle for Caen and the Falaise Pocket.

2 North of the village of Cintheaux, the Bretteville-sur-Laize Canadian War Cemetery contains 2,958 WW2 burials, the majority Canadian, and 87 of them unidentified.

3 The only Polish cemetery in France lies on the crossroad from Grainville–Langannerie to Urville, a few miles south of Caen. These fallen are primarily those of Polish 1st Armoured Division who fought during the Battle of Normandy in August 1944.

4 The Normandy American Cemetery contains the graves of 9,387 American war dead, most of whom lost their lives in the fighting on the beaches and during the D-Day landings and subsequent battles.

5 Michael Wittmann, his crew (Hirschel radio; Reimers, driver; Wagner, observer; Weber, loader), and 21,000 other Germans who fell fighting in Normandy are at La Cambe military cemetery maintained by the *Volksbund Deutsche Kriegsgräberfürsorge* (German War Graves Commission).

Key to Map Symbols

MILITARY MAP SYMBOLS

AAA	ARMOR	ARMY AIR FORCES	ARTILLERY	CAVALRY (MECZ)	ENGINEERS	INFANTRY
MEDICAL	SIGNALS	TANK DESTROYER	TRANSPORTATION	AIRBORNE AAA	AIRBORNE ARTILLERY	AIRBORNE INFANTRY

SQUAD	●	COMPANY, TROOP, BATTERY, AIR FORCE FLIGHT	I	BRIGADE, COMBAT COMMAND OF ARMORED DIVISION, OR AIR FORCE WING	X
SECTION	● ●	BATTALION, CAVALRY SQUADRON AIR FORCE SQUADRON	II	DIVISION OR COMMAND OF AN AIR FORCE	X X
PLATOON	● ● ●	REGIMENT OR GROUP, COMBAT TEAM (WITH ABBREVIATION CT FOLLOWING IDENTIFYING NUMERAL)	III	CORPS OR AIR FORCE	X X X
				ARMY	X X X X
				GROUP OF ARMIES	X X X X X

EXAMPLES

1 ⊠ 502
1st Bn 502nd PIR

Ⅱ
△23
OBSERVATION POST, 23rd INFANTRY

xx
⊠ 5
COMMAND POST, 5th INFANTRY

502
—III—
506
BOUNDARY BETWEEN 502nd AND 506th PIR

Two memorials between Burcy and Chendollé remember Operation Bluecoat. The first is to the "Normons"—a battlegroup made up of 1st Bn, Norfolk Regt (BR 3rd Inf Div), and 3rd Monmouthshire Regt (11th Armd Div)—who fought off attacks by 10th SS-Pz Div Frundsberg at some cost. The other is to Cpl Sidney "Basher" Bates who was awarded a posthumous VC for his courage during the action. The Normons success owed much to their artillery support, both British and American.

Bibliography

Online

http://the.shadock.free.fr/Surviving_Panzers. html Go to this site if you want any info on surviving AFVs.

https://forum.axishistory.com is a brilliant source of information.

Reynolds, Maj Gen Michael: "Poles in the West: Fighting in the Falaise Pocket" from http://warfarehistorynetwork.com/. Much of the information for the map on p. 44 was taken from a map in this article.

Traces of War (http://en.tracesofwar.com) is a fount of knowledge about memorials, fortifications, cemeteries, points of interest, awards: definitely worth checking out.

Books

Blumenson, Martin: *The European Theater of Operations: Breakout and Pursuit* (United States Army in World War II); Department of the Army, 1961.

Bradley, Omar N.: *A Soldier's Story*; Henry Holt, 1951.

Brisset, Jean: *The Charge of the Bull*; Bates Books, 1989.

Ellis, John: *Brute Force*; Andre Deutsch,

Ford, Ken: *Campaign 149 Falaise 1944 Death of an Army*; Osprey, 2005.

Hart, Stephen: *Battlezone Normandy 13 Road to Falaise*; Alan Sutton, 2004.

Hart, Stephen: *Campaign 294 Operation Totalize 1944*; Osprey, 2016.

Hastings, Max: *Overlord*; Michael Joseph, 1984.

Latawski, Paul: *Battlezone Normandy 14 Falaise Pocket*; Alan Sutton, 2004.

Palamountain, Edgar W. I.: *Taurus Pursuant A History of 11th Armoured Division*; 11th Armoured Division, 1946.